Catch This!

Thwack! It's a high-fly ball. Will it get over the fence? Follow the path of the ball to see if anyone can make the catch.

Illustrated by Brian White

3

Fido Funnies

Illustrated by Rich Powell

What did the dog say to the car?
"Hey, you're in my barking spot!"

What did the spy name her dog?
Snoopy.

What does a dog call his father?
Paw.

What is a dog's favorite movie?
Jurassic Bark.

What is the first thing a dog learns in school?
The arfabet.

Tommy: Why is your dog wearing glasses?
Tanya: Because contacts bother his eyes.

What dog loves to take bubble baths?
A shampoodle.

Illustrated by Kelly Kennedy

Crab Walk

This hermit crab needs a new shell. Can you find the path that will take him to his new home?

Start

Finish

Illustrated by Mattia Cerato

On the Ball!

Here's a pop quiz about "America's favorite pastime."
Circle your answers and see if you can knock this out of the ballpark.

1. In baseball, an "E" stands for what?
   a. Excellent
   b. Error
   c. Time to eat

2. Where does a pitcher warm up?
   a. A cowpen
   b. A bullpen
   c. A ranch

3. If you "swing and miss," what do you get?
   a. A strike
   b. A ball
   c. A sore arm

4. During what inning is "Take Me Out to the Ballpark" traditionally sung?
   a. 7th
   b. 8th
   c. 1st

5. If you're keeping score in baseball, what does "K" mean?
   a. Walk
   b. Strikeout
   c. Knobby Knees

6. If you "choke up" on a bat, what are you doing?
   a. Moving your hands up on the bat
   b. Moving your hands down on the bat
   c. Hurting the bat

7. The Little League Baseball World Series is held in which state?
   a. New York
   b. Pennsylvania
   c. None. There is no such thing.

Answers: 1. b, 2. b, 3. a, 4. a, 5. b, 6. a, 7. b

Illustrated by Bob Ostrom

Dog Run

Buster wants to meet up with his friends at the dog park. Can you help him sniff out the one trail that will take him there?

Illustrated by Mike Moran

White as Snow

The polar bear cannot be beat.
He's fond of arctic ice and sleet.
And when you see a mound of snow,
You say, "My, my, where did he go?"

by Carol Murray

Letter Drop

Only six of the letters in the top line will work their way through this maze to land in the numbered squares at the bottom. When they get there, they will spell out the answer to the riddle.

A C H B E R A O R R L D E

1 2 3 4 5 6

What do you call a flamingo at the North Pole?

___ ___ ___ ___ ___ ___
1   2   3   4   5   6

Illustrated by Jim Paillot

A Corny Quiz

The answer to each clue below contains the word CORN. How many can you figure out before it gets too corny?

Illustrated by Dave Clegg

1. A "baby" oak tree   __CORN

2. Where two walls meet   CORN__ __

3. Movie snack   __ __ __CORN

4. Mythical creature with hooves and one horn   __ __ __CORN

5. Halloween treat   __ __ __ __ __ CORN

6. A part of the eye   CORN__ __

7. A trumpet's "cousin"   CORN__ __

8. A football player position   CORN__ __ __ __ __ __

Illustrated by David Coulson

A Maize Maze

It might be corny, but it's fun. Can you help Daisy and Devon find their way through the cornfield maze?

Illustrated by Paul Richer

What's on the Wall?

Climb on up and look around. Use letters in the words ROCK CLIMBING WALL to spell new, shorter words. For example, the words CRAB and CLAM are both hiding in there. What other words can you round up?

ROCK CLIMBING WALL

crab

clam

Rock It

These rock climbers got their ropes tangled. Can you set them straight? Follow each rope from the climber on the mountain to find out who his or her partner is.

Illustrated by Jim Paillot

Bug Belly Laughs

What are caterpillars afraid of?
Dog-erpillars.

What kind of bug tells time?
A clockroach.

Passenger on plane: Those people down there look like ants!
Flight attendant: They are ants. We haven't left the ground yet.

Knock, knock.
Who's there?
Gnats.
Gnats who?
Gnats not a bit funny.

What did the bee say when it returned to the hive?
"*Honey, I'm home!*"

How do fireflies start a race?
Ready, Set, Glow!

What do you call a nervous cricket?
A jitterbug.

Why don't fleas catch cold?
Because they are always in fur coats.

Meet the Beetles

Mingo is meeting up with his friends. They've all made it to the middle of the maze. Can you help Mingo find his way there?

Illustrated by Mattia Cerato

Hockey Homes

It's a hockey night in . . . what city? Can you match each city with the name of its professional hockey team? Even you're not a hockey hound, give this quiz your best shot.

Boston   Penguins

Chicago   Redwings

Dallas   Bruins

Detroit   Lightning

Los Angeles   Flyers

Philadelphia   Kings

Pittsburgh   Blackhawks

Tampa Bay   Stars

Illustrated by Kelly Kennedy

The Puck Stops Here

Illustrated by Scott Burroughs

Syd is trying to score the game-winning goal. Can you help her find the right path to the net? The symbols will tell you which way to move.

Move 1 space up

Move 1 space right

Move 1 space left

Move 1 space down

Path 1	Path 2	Path 3	Path 4	Path 5	Path 6

15

 # Dig In!

Hungry for some fun? Try out these yummy tongue twisters. Can you say each three times fast?

Greek grapes.

Celia slurped spiced cider.

The beagle brought bagels for breakfast.

Many moose munch much mush.

Paul picked a particular pickle.

Criscrossed crispy piecrust.

Seven lemon lollipops.

Straw Twister

Everyone's enjoying an ice-cream soda. But who is drinking which one? Follow each straw to find out!

Illustrated by Jim Paillot

Strive for Five

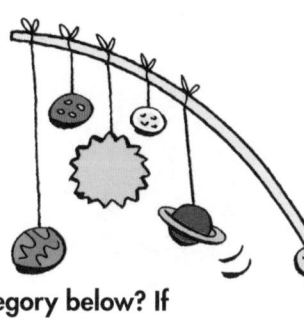

Can you name five things in each category below? If you do, give yourself a high five!

Breeds of dogs

_____
_____
_____
_____
_____

Planets

_____
_____
_____
_____
_____

Names that start with D

_____
_____
_____
_____
_____

Fruits

_____
_____
_____
_____

Flavors of ice cream

_____
_____
_____
_____

Five Sides

Fitz's favorite number is five, and he has just finished drawing a maze with five sides. Help him get out of this perplexing pentagon, and when you're done, see if you can spot five sets of five things in this scene.

START

FINISH

Illustrated by Susan Miller

Art Antics

Illustrated by Rich Powell

What is a cow's favorite painting?
Moona Lisa.

What is an art teacher's favorite fruit?
Crayonberries.

How does a tree draw a person?
It makes a stick figure.

Why was the artist so popular?
He could always draw a crowd.

How do artists greet one another?
Yellow!

Brushstrokes

Which brush painted each word?

Illustrated by Jim Steck

Two Left Feet

Two left feet?
It doesn't matter.
Turn the music on and start.
Dancing's less about the feet
And so much more about the heart.

by Eileen Spinelli

Illustrated by Rémy Simard

Letter Drop

Only six of the letters in the top line will work their way through this maze to land in the numbered squares at the bottom. When they get there, they will spell out the answer to the riddle.

R H A I P R O H C O K O P

1 2 3 4 5 6

What is a rabbit's favorite kind of music?

23

To the Tune of
the Moon

The answer to each clue below rhymes with the word "moon."
If you can get them all, we might swoon.

1. A summer month   _ _ _ _

2. When the sun is highest in the sky   _ _ _ _

3. A natural hill of sand   _ _ _ _

4. In a short amount of time   _ _ _ _

5. Use it to eat soup   _ _ _ _ _

6. A dried plum   _ _ _ _ _

7. Hot-air _____   _ _ _ _ _ _ _

8. The farthest planet from the sun   _ _ _ _ _ _ _

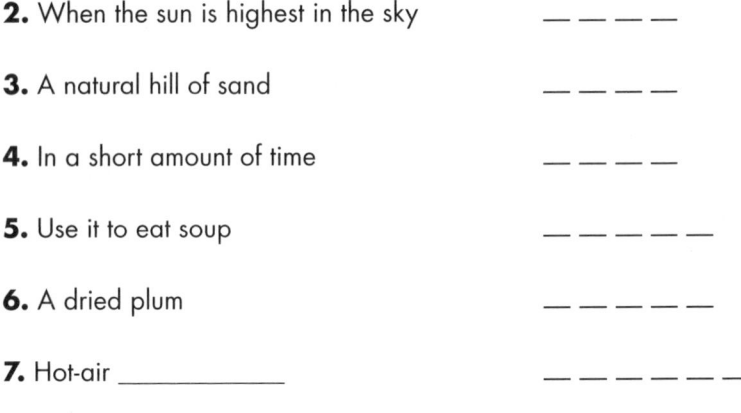

Answers: 1. June, 2. Noon, 3. Dune, 4. Soon, 5. Spoon, 6. Prune, 7. Balloon, 8. Neptune

Moonlighting

Trevor and his family took a hike in the moonlight.
Now they need help finding the way back to their campsite.
Can you find the path that will take them to their tents?

Start

Finish

Illustrated by Paul Richer

Match Batch

Can you match each clue to a pair of rhyming words that describes it? We did the first to get you started.

1. Rubber reptile

2. Squished baseball cap

3. Rabbit comedian

4. Intelligent insects

5. Happy canine

6. 16-year-old who showered

7. Brave primate

8. Sunburned noggin

9. Stinky sandwich shop

10. Child who lives on a fancy boat

Spunky monkey

Smelly deli

Clean teen

Fake snake

Red head

Yacht tot

Wise flies

Jolly collie

Flat hat

Funny bunny

Illustrated by Jack Desrocher

Jelly Belly

Help Little Lisa find the path that will lead her safely past Jelly Belly to pal Big Betty.

START

FINISH

Illustrated by T. F. Cook

Tangled up in T

Try out these T-riffic tongue twisters!
Can you say each three times fast without tripping over your tongue?

Tiny turtles tried on tutus.

Tacky tractor trailer trucks.

Talented tarantulas taught tennis.

Twenty-two tired toads tied twine.

Twelve tigers twirled twelve twigs.

The *T. Rex* tripped twice.

Truly rural train.

Tammy tried to tie Thomas's twisty tie.

Tree Trek

Willow's friends built a brand-new tree house. She can't wait to climb aboard! Can you help Willow find the one path across her neighborhood that will take her there?

Start

Finish

Illustrated by Mike Moran

What a Ham!

Hamster isn't the only word with HAM in its name. Use the clues below to find more. Get them all, and you'll be the c**ham**pion!

1. Put dirty clothes in this.   HAM__ __ __

2. Use this to pound nails.   HAM__ __ __

3. Popular sandwich at cookouts   HAM__ __ __ __ __ __

4. Wash your hair with this.   __HAM__ __ __

5. Type of cracker used in s'mores   __ __ __HAM

6. A swinging outdoor "bed"   HAM__ __ __ __

7. A green national symbol of Ireland   __HAM__ __ __ __

8. This type of lizard can change colors   __HAM__ __ __ __ __

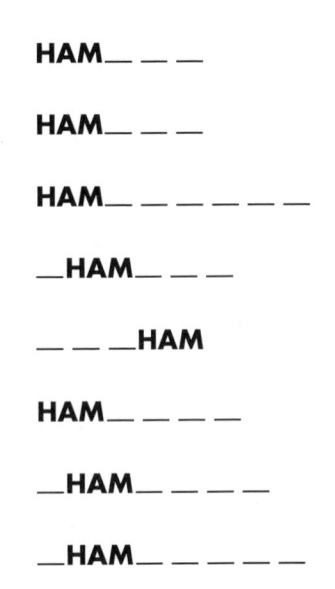

Illustrated by Kelly Kennedy

Inner Tubes

This hamster can't wait to chow down. But there is only one path that will lead him to his treats. Can you help him find it?

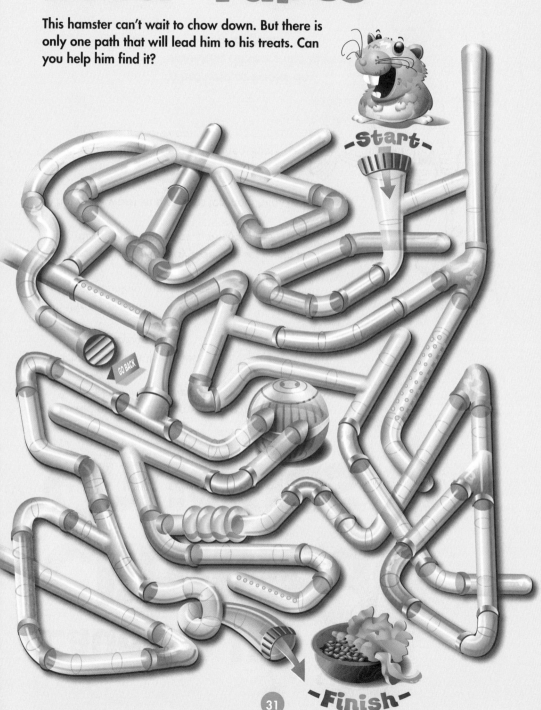

-Start-

GO BACK

-Finish-

Laugh it UP: Climbing Chuckles

Illustrated by Kelly Kennedy

What did one mountain say to the other mountain?
"Meet me in the valley."

Which mountain is the laziest?
Mount Ever-rest.

What is a volcano?
A mountain with hiccups.

Why wouldn't the hills play hide-and-seek with the mountains?
Because the mountains always "peak."

What is the worst time of year for mountain climbing?
The fall.

Why don't mountains get cold in the winter?
They wear snow caps.

**What kind of books do
mountain climbers like to read?**
Cliffhangers.

Illustrated by David Coulson

Uphill Climb

Rocky is almost to the summit of the cliff. Can you help him find his footing the rest of the way? Just one path will take him to the top.

Finish

Start

Illustrated by Paul Richer

Round and Round

Can you get your head around this puzzle? Unscramble each set of letters to spell something that's ROUND.

1. BLAL   <u>b a l l</u>

2. RIET   _ _ _ _

3. NEPYN   _ _ _ _ _

4. REATH   _ _ _ _ _

5. RAMBEL   _ _ _ _ _ _

6. GRANOE   _ _ _ _ _ _

7. LUAH OPOH   _ _ _ _   _ _ _ _

8. FLUL OMNO   _ _ _ _   _ _ _ _

Answers: 1. Ball; 2. Tire; 3. Penny; 4. Earth; 5. Marble; 6. Orange; 7. Hula hoop; 8. Full moon

Flip for It

Chase just flipped his flying disc to his faithful friend, Otto. Can you find the path the disc will take to reach Otto?

Start

Finish

Illustrated by Mike Moran

35

Horse Sense

Can you tell a Clydesdale from a clodhopper? Each pair below contains one real horse and one faker. Saddle up, and see how many real horses you can circle.

Mustang **OR** Chevy?

Appaloosa **OR** Appatighta?

Thoroughcake **OR** Thoroughbred?

Straight **OR** Curly?

Fire Horse **OR** Shire Horse?

Missouri Fox Trotter **OR** Mississippi Mink Runner?

Bulging **OR** Belgian?

Lipizzan **OR** Tarzan

Illustrated by Kelly Kennedy

Marble Mining

Illustrated by Dave Klug

What can you find in a game of marbles? You tell us! Use the letters in the words GAME OF MARBLES to spell new, shorter words. For example, the words *EAGLE* and *SOAR* are in there. See how many other words you can find.

GAME OF MARBLES

eagle

soar

_____

_____

_____

_____

_____

_____

_____

_____

_____

_____

_____

_____

_____

_____

Mind Your Marbles!

Two marbles are about to go on a roll through this marvelous marble maze. Where will the **red** one come out? Where will the **blue** one come out?

Illustrated by Marc Nadel

39

Basketball Funnies

What is a basketball player's favorite kind of cheese?
Swish.

What does outer space have in common with basketball?
They both have shooting stars.

Why wasn't Cinderella good at basketball?
She ran away from the ball.

Why don't fish like to play basketball?
They are afraid of the net.

What do you do if a basketball court gets flooded?
Call in the subs.

When is a baby good at basketball?
When it's dribbling.

What do pigs do when they play basketball?
They hog the ball.

Two Points

Marissa and Matthew are meeting at the rec center to shoot hoops. Can you help each of them find a path to the court?

Start

Start

Finish

Illustrated by Jim Paillot

41

Silly Books

We found a bunch of fun books about space and other science topics. Check them out below. Which would you most like to read?

Floating Furniture by Auntie Gravity

Distance to the Moon by Myles A. Way

Electricity by Sir Kit

All about Atoms by Molly Cule

How to Save the Planet by Reese Ikle

Strong Bones by Cal C. Uhm

The Water's Surface by Al Gee

Shapes by Paul E. Gone

Reading Space

Do you know what astronauts like to read? Follow each line from a letter to a blank space and write the letter in that space. When you are finished, you will have the answer.

Illustrated by Mike Moran

Taking Turns

One by one they get in line,
Flippers flapping, black on white.
One dives in, then each in turn.
Who knew penguins were polite?

"Stay in line and wait your turn,"
Says our teacher at the zoo.
Penguin-watching makes me think
They must have a teacher, too!

by Elizabeth Glann

Illustrated by Richard Powell

Penguin Path

This penguin is hungry! Can you help him slip and slide down a path that leads into the water so he can fish for food? Be careful not to crash into any other penguins.

Illustrated by Dan McGeehan

Start

Finish

Toothy Tongue Twisters

Think you can say these tongue twisters three times fast?

Illustrated by Kelly Kennedy

They threw three thick things.

Thirty-three thin thermometers.

Tom threw Tim three thumbtacks.

I thought of thinking of thanking you.

Ted threw Fred thirty-three free throws.

Those toes aren't these toes.

This Thanksgiving, please thaw the turkey.

Thelma sings the theme song.

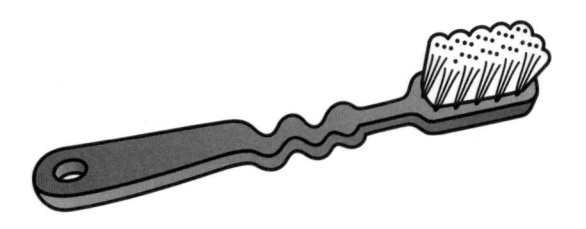

Illustrated by Rita Lascaro

Squeeze Play

Tessa, Owen, Olivia, and Theo have made a mess! Follow the paths and see if you can figure out which tube of toothpaste belongs to which kid.

Amuse Me

What will you find in an amusement park? Thrilling rides, sweet treats, and lots of words! Use the letters in AMUSEMENT PARK to spell new, shorter words. For example, the words SUMMER and SPARK are in there. How many others can you find?

AMUSEMENT PARK

summer

spark

Log Jamming

Grab your wetsuit! This log is about to take the plunge.
Can you steer it smoothly all the way to FINISH without
getting soaked? Just one path will take you there.

49

Illustrated by Steve Skelton

Finish

Test Your Movie IQ

Are you a fan of giant screens? Do you crave buttered popcorn? Then you should take this quiz about the movies. Try to answer every question, and you'll be a star!

1. Which word is not another term for a movie?
   a. Film
   b. Flick
   c. Trick

2. Most movies in the U.S. are created in which California City?
   a. Hollywood
   b. San Francisco
   c. Santa Barbara

3. What is the movie industry in India known as?
   a. Dollywood
   b. Bollywood
   c. Indy Films

4. People without speaking roles who appear in the background of a movie are called what?
   a. Extras
   b. Additionals
   c. College students

5. What year was the first "talkie"–a movie with sound–released?
   a. 1897
   b. 1927
   c. 1777

6. Which U.S. president was also a movie star?
   a. George W. Bush
   b. Ronald Reagan
   c. George Washington

7. What is the name for the highest American award in the movie industry?
   a. Oscar
   b. Tony
   c. Mickey Mouse

Movie Maze

Steven is meeting his friends for a movie. But first he has to find the movie theater! Can you help him find the one path that will take him there? Hurry, it's almost showtime!

Start

Finish

Illustrated by Mike Moran

Z Zz

Ants

Each single crumb
grows legs
and sneaks

a w a y to feed an army.

Illustrated by Stacy Curtis

—Kristin Dempsey

Ant Eater

Can you help this ant find its way to the food? Just one path will take it there. Try not to get too antsy along the way!

Finish

Start

Illustrated by Mattia Cerato

Do These Bowling Jokes Strike You as Funny?

What are old bowling balls used as?
Marbles for elephants.

Liam: What is the quietest sport?
Nora: Bowling, of course. You can hear a pin drop!

Why do tires get upset when they go bowling?
Because they never make strikes, just spares.

What kind of cats like to go bowling?
Alley cats.

What did the bowling ball say to the pins?
"Don't stop me! I'm on a roll."

Ruby: Why is bowling better than baseball?
Jack: Why?
Ruby: Because you can get three strikes and you're not out!

What is stranger than seeing a catfish?
Seeing a fishbowl.

Emma weighs 78 pounds. She has to take three one-pound bowling pins across a bridge that will hold only 80 pounds. How can she do it?
Follow each line from a letter to a blank space and write the letter in that space. When you are finished, you will have the answer.

Illustrated by Mike Moran

Illustrated by Dave Clegg

Sole Searching

Step into this maze at START and make your way to
FINISH without backtracking or repeating your route.
Pass the numbers in order along the way.

START

FINISH

Illustrated by Elizabeth Carpenter

EARS to You

Bite into this maze at START and nibble your way to FINISH without backtracking or repeating any routes. Stop at the five numbers in order along the way. When you're done, take a look at the whole maze and you'll find a surprise.

START

FINISH

Illustrated by Elizabeth Carpenter

Answers

1 Crab Walk

3 Catch This!

5 Dog Run

7 Letter Drop

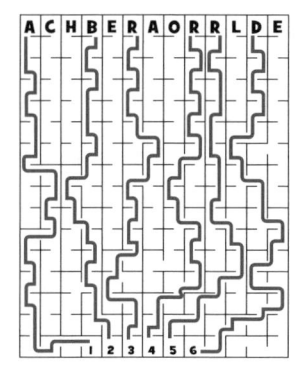

What do you call a flamingo at the North Pole? A BRRRD

9 A Maize Maze

11 Rock It

13 Meet the Beetles

Answers

15 The Puck Stops Here

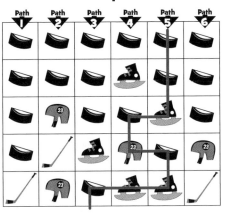

17 Straw Twister

19 Five Sides

There are five flowers, squirrels, birds, ants (by the garbage can), and pieces of chalk (including the one in Fitz's hand).

21 Brushstrokes

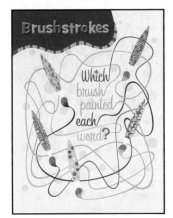

23 Letter Drop

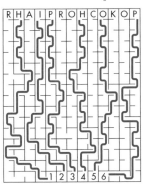

What is a rabbit's favorite kind of music? HIP HOP

25 Moonlighting

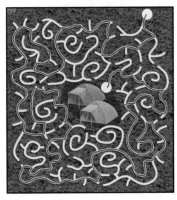

Answers

27 Jelly Belly

29 Tree Trek

31 Inner Tubes

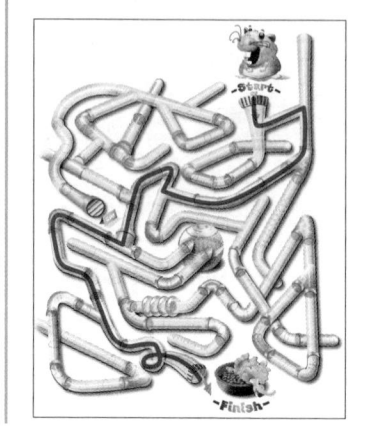

33 Uphill Climb

35 Flip for It

37 The Mane Route

39 Mind Your Marbles!

Answers

41 Two Points

43 Reading Space

45 Penguin Path

47 Squeeze Play

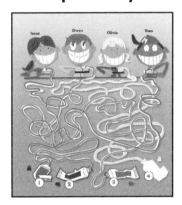

49 Log Jamming

51 Movie Maze

Answers

53 Ant Eater

55 Weight a Second!

56–57 Sole Searching

58–59 EARS to You

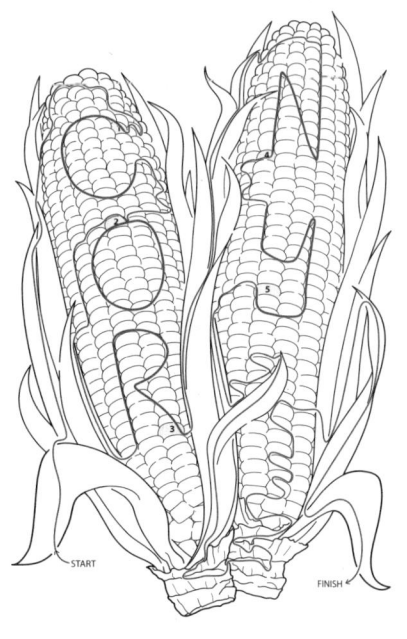